Ravens Moon

A Poetry Collection

C. Churchill

Copyright 2020 C. Churchill

"Ravens Moon"

All rights reserved. No part of this publication may be reproduced, distributed, or conveyed, without express written permission from the Author

C. Churchill

Cover Art and photography within by C. Churchill

Also, by C. Churchill

Wildflower Tea

Petals of the Moon

Racing Ravens

Chasing Pines

Mirror Mirror

What is magick?

or is it magic?

Are you new here?

I am

I have spent the last several months alone on this planet and most of that time was spent alone in the center of a dark forest.

These poems reflect what I learned about magick.

Ravens Moon was born of part purpose part passion
After creating several collections of poetry, I thought about my process and realized while writing and reading poetry I have always spoken the words aloud
Most of my pieces resembled spell work and I write with a heavy influence of nature.
Growing up part Native American, part Irish my roots contained magick spanning several centuries. Although I have recently begun my exploration into traditional ways of magick I can say without a doubt it has been in my life, as long as I can remember.
This collection of poetry was created with the awareness that I am new to the traditional set of rules for magick and also aware that energy and the universe can be powerful tools for anyone and at any place in their journey with magick.
From the time I was a small child I would venture into the thick forest alone and sit for hours just watching and listening as my heart learned to trust nature. I was fortunate enough to find solace in a world where many people would be scared to venture alone.

I have spent the majority of a year in the deep forest where I was free to write this collection in complete solitude. I have set this collection up in a way where the poems are placed on the facing page and on the first page an explanation and a list of enhancements. After all, when words are read aloud, they become more powerful and who is to say the flame of a candle or holding a crystal might enhance things further. I am new here, but I have learned what I am naturally drawn to when bringing intentions into fruition and releasing them into the universe.
I am not going to get into any specific realm of divinity nor will I go deeply into things about religion and practice that I do not understand, because that is not my place.
I will express to you however that I believe fully in energy and the universe and I am a firm believer that what you put out comes back to you.
You will not find dark magic in these verses, but you will find kindness to yourself and others. Good tidings and clarifications.
I am still asking questions and learning quite a bit and I feel comfortable spinning some verse filled with good intentions out into the world.
I do hope you enjoy and who knows maybe this will lead you down a path you never thought you would be ready for. I now invite you to discover the magick.

Letting Go
Letting go of Worry	12
Letting go of Fear	14
Letting go of Want	16
Letting go of Guilt	18
Letting go of Anger	20
Letting go of the Past	22
Letting go of Those Who No Longer Serve Us	24

Protection
Safe Home	28
Hex Breaker	30
Protect Against False Glamor	32
Warrior Protection	34
Protection of Mind	36
Protect against Enemies	38

Love
Attracting Love	42
See the Truth in Love	44
Selflove	46
Bring Love Back	48
Happiness in Love	50
Love thy Neighbor	52

Luck and Success

Success Within	56
Lucky Charm	58
Windfall	60
Job Success	62
Jumpstart Motivation	64
Attract Success	66
Fortune	68

Health and Home

Whole Spirit	72
Restful Sleep	74
Nightmares No More	76
Health of a Loved One	78
Safe Travels	80
Safe Home	82

Blessings

Full Moon Blessing	86
New Moon Blessing	88
Blessing for Home	90
Blessing for a Clear Path	92
Blessing from Afar	94

Clean slate for believing

I have riddled my mind with research from books and from friends who have been on their journey in magick for decades. I wanted to explore my magick but my head was filled with so many beliefs and traditions that it just was spinning with no clear path to begin. I sat in the forest awhile and certain words began to appear and from my soul came the words.

Suggested enhancement:

Sit in complete solitude in a place you trust and completely feel connected. Take deep healing breaths until you find your calm.

Remember the three C's as you read the poems in this collection
Calm: Breaths
Create: A focused state
Connect: To the elements around you

Maple oak birch and pine
Virgin forest of divine
Let me free of these boots
So I may walk barefoot
Among these roots
Bring me back
From modern times
To be reborn
Of nature's lines

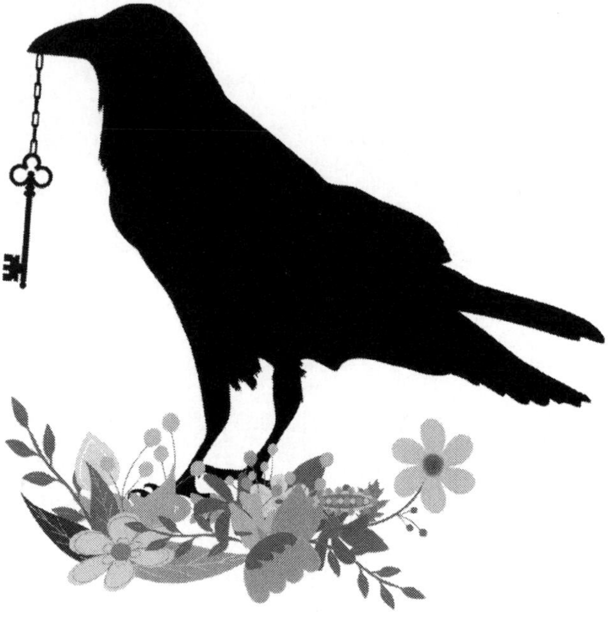

LETTING GO

After letting go the words started to flow and I realized letting go of not only preconceived thoughts and notions but also some baggage was going to be necessary so I started to write pieces that would lift the weight of certain things in my world.

Letting Go of Worry

Suggested Enhancements

Stand facing the sun and repeat these words as you lift your hands to the sky,

Letting Go of Worry

Allow my thoughts
To no longer wander
Lingering in
worries ponder

Take my hands
Heavy in wait
Lift them high
Long and straight

As I raise them
to the skies
Touching light
Not the lies

Let me release
Worry filled days
So, I may breathe
In light filled ways

Letting Go of Fear

Suggested Enhancements

Strike a match
light a candle
blow it out so that the smoke
travels out a nearby window
or light it outside.

Letting Go of Fear

In this match I yield the power
To light this wick
Flame to flower
I let go of this fear
No longer haunting
My mind so clear
No longer daunting
Let this ghost
Curl in smoke
Away the wind carry
These words to invoke

Letting Go of Want

Suggested Enhancements

Clear your mind from all you see and focus on a simple item like the flame of a candle or a crystal held in your hand

Letting Go of Want

Simple breaths
Simple needs
Make me see
And believe

All this want
Before my eyes
Is only time
Wrapped in lies

Simple breaths
Simple needs
Make me see
It is all I need

Letting Go of Guilt

Suggested Enhancements

In a bowl of collected water either from rain or from tap swirl the water clockwise and while repeating the words. If you charge water under a full mon it will be enhanced further.

Letting Go of Guilt

Swirl in waters
Deep with silt
Banish my heart
Free of guilt

Be it reed, wand
Or fingertip
The ripples release
Guilts ownership

Swirl in waters
Clear to pass
Allowing the leaving
Of guilt from path

Letting Go of Anger

Suggested Enhancements

Write whatever you are angry about on a piece of paper and fold it three times. Light the paper and let it burn in a firesafe bowl or hearth. After it has burned douse with water.

Letting Go of Anger

Sticks and stones
Heavy these bones
As fires blaze in mind

Waves of calm
Wash these teeth
Release them from this grind

To speak a language
Of love, not hate
A smile free and kind

Let this anger
Leave me now
My faith has come aligned

Letting Go of the Past

Suggested Enhancements

With any mirror to look in hold a key in your hand and focus on the cold metal instead of your reflection.

Letting Go of the Past

As I glance to where I have been
I hold these keys
Cold metal on skin
Reminding me
We are no longer engaged
I leave my past
And turn the page

Letting Go of Those Who No Longer Serve Us

Suggested Enhancements

On a plate pour some sand or dirt and draw the name of the person you wish to no longer to be directly involved in your life.

Letting Go of Those Who No Longer Serve Us

I scribe your name
In this sand
And grains fall away

You have no power
Left in here
You can no longer stay

This cage is no longer
 where I live
And my mind will no longer sway

I blow this sand
Erasing you
So, I may start my day

PROTECTION

There is no such thing as too much protection. In dark times it is not uncommon to want to feel more protected against various things.

Safe Home

Suggested Enhancements

Light a blue candle somewhere near the front entrance of your home or light a sage cleansing bundle. As always use extreme caution with any open flame. After the candle has been lit and the words have been read extinguish the candle. if you are using sage walk clockwise through your home cleansing it with smoke as you read. Open doors and windows to release the smoke.

Safe Home

Peace is welcome
As are friends
Before these walls
Evil ends

Keepers watch
Our spirits soar
Protecting windows
And these doors

We sleep safely
Under wings
Of sage and promise
And new day brings

Hex breaker

Suggested Enhancement

Stand outside and gather some leaves that have fallen. Crunch leaves and let them fall all around you in a circle.

Hex Breaker

I call to you
As I touch this earth
Please relieve
Any hex or curse

These leaves have fallen
To give new growth
In this circle
All evil smote

Protect Against False Glamour

Suggested Enhancements

Light a white candle.

Protect Against False Glamour

Winds of change
Bring cool sharp rain
Let this season
Unmask feign

Show true colors
Of those we know
So, we can protect
As they grow

A shield to flower
I call to thee
Let me be soft
In this truth I seek

Warrior protection

Suggested Enhancements

Calm your breathing and focus on your inner strength. Sit in a northerly direction.

Warrior Protection

I call to thee
North south east west
Protect the child within
Let her see no harm
As my warrior rises

I call to thee
Earth fire wind and water
Raise this warrior
To be battle ready

I call to thee
Sun moon stars and universe
Make right what has been wronged
A clear path
For warriors strong

Protection of Mind

Suggested Enhancements

On a simple scrap of paper write down what forces may be interrupting your calm state of mind. Focus on ridding them as you tear the paper to bits.

Protection of Mind

Let me go under duress
Let my mind seek its best
Protect against
Those not kind
Save my hearth
Save my mind
For this fire is not to consume
But light the future
Before the tomb
Save my heart
Before it blackens
Save my mind
from those attacking

Protect Against Enemies

Suggested Enhancements

Clear your mind of all things and focus on your enemies. Push those thoughts from focus to your breath exhale them into the universe.

Protect Against Enemies

They do not know
The seeds they sow
They are unaware
The karma they bear

They will not sidle
When rains come idle
See them through
But protect us too

Because they are not to trust
But filled with lust
For power and might
Is a golden knight

And protection is in need
When our enemies turn to greed

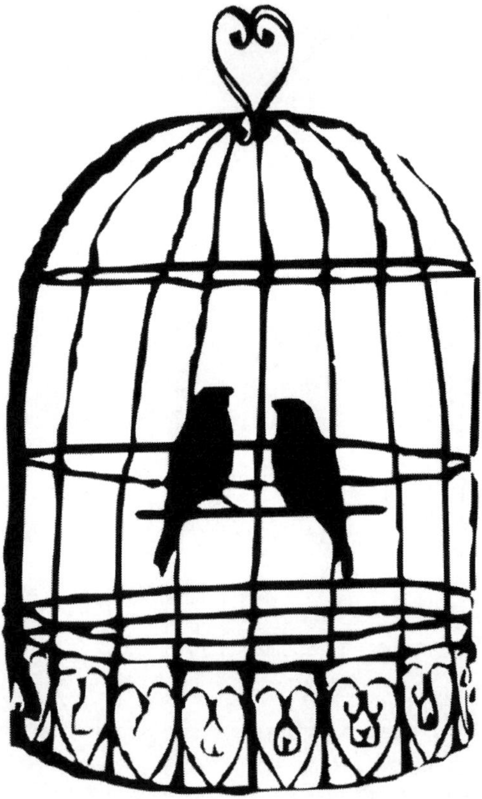

LOVE

Attracting Love

Suggested enhancements

Take a flower and focus your intention as you pluck the petals and form a circle around a rose quartz crystal.

Attracting Love

I place these petals
Around my heart
Sending love,
A sweet, sweet start
May the pure see my soul
and in this garden
love will grow

See the Truth in Love

Suggested Enhancements

Write the name of the person you want to see the truth from and wrap it with some string. In a fireproof container light the paper and recite the words. With all dealings with flame use caution and extinguish properly.

See the Truth in Love

I held my heart
In loves sweet grace
But true as anything
I await faith

Tell me if this
Love is true
Banish those
That make me fool

Self-Love

Suggested Enhancements

Rub hands together to find a warmth within.

Self-Love

I lay my hands in fire
To bring back
Self loves desire
To cure my heart of this weak moment
To see myself as a warrior
I lay my hands upon my soul
To see that this love can grow
Darkness is no longer my shield
Bring the light to my yield
In times of darkness
I will prevail
Because my light
Is stronger than any ail

Bring Love Back

Suggested Enhancements

Have a photo of your intended of write their name on a piece of paper and while reciting focus of your heart beating.

Bring Love Back

I sit in wait no longer
For this love has had time to ponder
Return this heart to its roots
Where we were kissed under moons
Where we found loves innate truth
Where we held each other's noon
Return this heart
To all splendor
Of what love holds and its endeavor
Return to me a love that is true
And if it is not let it run through

Happiness in Love

Suggested Enhancements

Rose Quartz is a handy tool to place on your heart when putting love intentions into the universe.

Happiness in Love

My petals have unfurled
To let love, begin its rule
Smiles and touch
Will be pleasant with luck
Let my heart absorb this glory
For happiness in love
Is my new story

Love thy Neighbor

Suggested Enhancements

We often tend to forget to wish those well that are seeking to harm but we must use our light to conquer hate. Try to bring your light to the surface and recite with as much light as you can.

Love thy Neighbor

I see what they have done
I scorn the ground they stand upon
But I will wish them well
As they live their own hell
My retort is not viable
While I sit and watch their demise
I wish them truth I wish them love
I wish they learn to stand above
Stand above hate
Stand above anger
I wish they could see farther than the danger
Give them healing that they deserve
To lift them out of the hell they have earned

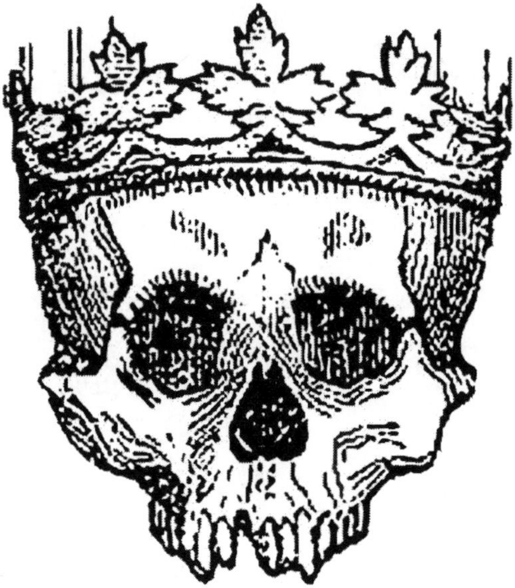

LUCK AND SUCCESS

Success Within

Suggested Enhancements

Focus on bringing your heart and mind together and imagine your future success

Success Within

There is fire in these veins
Whether the ash did try to claim
I am ready to use this force
To return
To my intended course
There is fire
Uncontrolled
I will use this as my source

Living in the past is not my course
I will see this fire
Grow large
I will be the one in charge

Lucky Charm

Suggested Enhancement

Any token or trinket that you deem lucky place in your pocket for three days' time.

Lucky Charm

Into my pocket
I place this charm
With all intention
To cause no harm

To bloom an energy
Of luck this day
For this charm
To light my way

Into my pocket
I place this charm
Feeling the love
As the world goes round

Charm of mine
Find a place
In my heart
I left you space

Windfall

Suggested Enhancement

Hold a coin in your palm and recite these words in a warm sunlit room.

Windfall

I stop and see
Riches are not meant for me
I ask the sky
Will the winds abide
To give a gift
I cannot provide
For in my soul
I need to find
Just a moment of less grief
A windfall necessary
For those who believe
In my heart
I know you are there
Because karma
Has a purse to share
I will return my gift tenfold
Because that is when our souls are filled

Job Success

Suggested Enhancements

Light a white candle to bring light into your view and extinguish to expel any lack of confidence.

Job Success

I have the tools
I have the scurry
Please let them see
I am worthy
I can do this job
To the best of my ability
And they will not be sorry
They gave me this identity

Jumpstart Motivation

Suggested Enhancement

Fill a cup with water and slowly pour the water into the dirt or a plant, anywhere there is growth.

Jumpstart Motivation

I have sat in dust for far too long
Watching others receive their crown
As my tears filled my cup
They have been building nonstop
I ask of thee to remove my bind
Let my soul breathe its fire
And become in kind
Success to come in this hour
And give me the heart to meet its follow

Attract Success

Suggested Enhancement

Repeat the words while wrapping a string around a rolled-up piece of paper money or write on a piece of paper what success you hope to attract and do the same.

Attract Success

Give me the eyes to see this future
Give me the tongue to speak in wisdom
Give me the hands to craft success
Give me the heart to make it blessed

Fortune

Suggested Enhancements

Any piece of metal or jewelry will do if it is important to you and flame proof. Light a candle and with extreme caution pass the object through the flame on a full moon night.

Fortune

A piece of gold, a trinket I share
Burn in a pyre
To make it bare
Cleanse it well under this moon
Full and bright
Ready to rule
I share this piece of my self
To bring good tidings
Of fortune and wealth

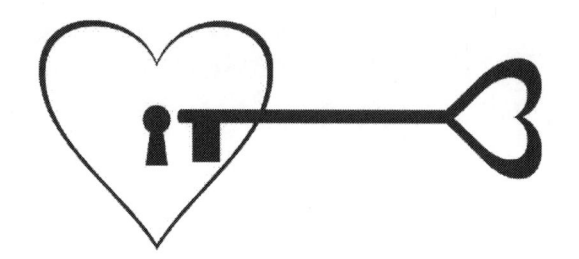

HEALTH AND HOME

Whole Spirit

Suggested Enhancement

Write on a piece of paper how you feel your spirit has fractured and what it would look like to be whole. Fold the three times. Place it in a fireproof dish and light it safely on fire till it burns to ash.

Whole Spirit

Pieces crack along the lines
Showing damage of the times
I bind this parchment
Once more than thrice
And burn to ash
Every splice
For my spirit
Is ready to be whole
Once again ready to soar

Restful Sleep

Suggested Enhancements

Use lavender oil on a sachet to place under your pillow.

Restful Sleep

Lavender fields
And poppy trains
Fill my nights
With restful dreams
For when I wake
I fear no task
Because my body
Has taken back
Sleep once in rare form
Now has landed
On this throne

Nightmares no more

Suggested Enhancements

Ready yourself for bed and leave a small light on during the night. It may be a nightlight or a light in another room.

Nightmares no more

As I close my eyes this night
I will ignore the haunt and fright
for these demons that enter this bed
Are far from real and in my head
How can I fear
Nightmares any longer
When I have given them
No power to be stronger
As I close my eyes this night
I am no longer afraid to fight
For I am the only demon in this bed
And everything else is just is just he said she said

Health of a Loved One

Suggested enhancements

Write on a piece of paper the name of the person you wish to have good health and wear it close to your heart for a night and a day.

Health of a loved one

Let this sickness travel light
Protecting my heart in the night
In the morning it shall slow
And find a way to no longer grow
As my hands light this fire
Love is stronger than most desire
In my heart this love is strong
And this sickness finally will be gone

Safe Travels

Suggested enhancements

Write on a piece of paper the name of the person you wish to have safe travels and wear it close to your heart for the length of the journey.

Safe Travels

A journey must be taken
Along roads that have been forsaken
Guide this travel with love and light
For it will be a long dark night
I place this tiding to my breast
As close to heart
And to be blessed

Safe Home

Suggested Enhancements

Light a white candle and focus on purifying your home. Make sure the candle is extinguished after you are done.

Safe Home

From roof to floor
And wall to door
A nest of safety
I do implore
Clear the evil from this place
For a home should be a safe space
From root to branch
And wind to willow
Allow only safety
To seed this pillow
So, dreams can heal and be carefree
In a home of safety, I ask this blessed be

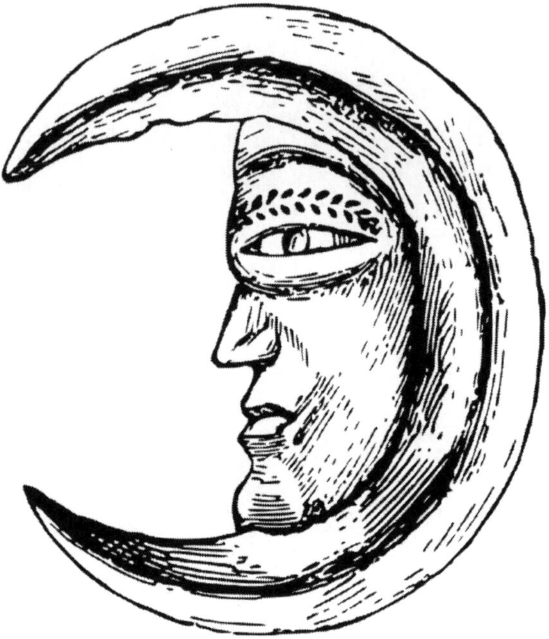

BLESSINGS

Full Moon Blessing

Suggested Enhancements

Take a bath or shower to cleanse yourself physically then recite the words while still bare under a full moon. Do not do this outside unless you legit live in a place that is warm enough and without people around.

Full Moon Blessing

Under this light
Full and bright
I thank thee
For blessings be

Under this night
Full and bright
I ask thee
To replenish me

New Moon Blessing

Suggested enhancements

New Moons are a time for new beginnings to shed the old and start anew. Think of what you need to start anew and speak them into the universe after reciting the words on the following page.

New Moon Blessing

Darkness veil
Cover me this night
A new beginning to pass
Next morning light
New moon to carry
Intentions forth
Until the next
New moon comes to course

Blessing for Home

Suggested Enhancements

Read the words on the next page out loud while traveling through your home.

Blessing for Home

Cleanse this house
Cleanse it free
Blessings to land
Every corner I see
Good wishes and tidings
Enter this home
For it is now blessed
Without scorn

Blessing for a Clear Path

Suggested enhancements

Using a feather wave in the air while reciting the words on the following page.

Blessing for a Clear Path

Mark these words
With wings of flight
Carry intention
Through the night
They will land
To mark this path
Clear of trouble
Clear of past

Blessing from Afar

Suggested enhancement

Write your person you wish to bless name on a piece of paper and wear it close to your heart.

Blessing from Afar

I know you are far away
But that does not lessen
How I pray
For you to have
A light this day
In my thoughts
You will stay
Blessings for you
I carry true

With all magick it is our belief in ourselves and the energy of the universe that carries our intention. The words and enhancements in this collection are a mere suggestion.

About the Author

C. Churchill lives in Northern Michigan and she can be found hiking in the forests or along the shores of the Great Lakes enjoying nature and gathering inspiration.

More books by C. Churchill

Wildflower Tea
Petals of the Moon
Racing Ravens
Chasing Pines
Mirror Mirror

All her books can be found on Amazon and most online booksellers.

Blessed Be

Manufactured by Amazon.ca
Bolton, ON